The Big Fat Red Juicy Apple Cook Book

Edited by Judith Bosley

Cover design by Gary Nowak

Airbrush Artist—Joseph P. Baldino

Illustrations by Jill Ellen Parling

L.E.B. INC.
Livonia, Michigan 48150

Library of Congress Catalog Card Number 84-81450

ISBN 0-930809-04-1

L.E.B. INC.
27599 Schoolcraft
Livonia, Michigan 48150

Everyone loved our first BIG RED FAT JUICY APPLE COOK BOOK, and we sold out, right down to the bottom of the barrel. We asked the finest apple cooks we could find for their favorite apple dishes, and compiled this new edition for you. We saved the best old standbys from the first book, and added many luscious new dishes. An effort has been made to include many sugar free recipes that are still "sweet as pie." Now our back cover is an apple too, and both covers are coated so that fingerprints and spilled drops will wipe right off. Maybe you'll want to hang it in a handy spot in your kitchen.

So, pile the kids in the car and visit a cider mill, orchard or roadside apple market. Pick a peck of Ida Reds, Golden Delicious, or whichever variety makes you drool, and a jug of cider. Then pick up this book. Try #12, Apple 'N Chicken Salad, and serve it with Spiced Apple Muffins, #43. Some dreary winter day, cheer up your family or guests with Apple-Cheese Torte, #74, a recipe given to me by a gourmet cook, "just in case you ever redo your apple book."

From one apple lover to another, ENJOY!

APPLE FACTS

What you don't know about apples will seldom hurt you a bit. Sure, there are the experts that know and use certain varieties for certain dishes, and you will too. But all apples are good to eat out of hand, depending on your taste for sweet or tart, soft or firm. And there are many, many varieties good for all purposes. A few of them are:

McINTOSH   **JONATHAN**
IDA RED   **CORTLAND**

For pies and baking

NORTHERN SPY   **WINESAP**
WEALTHY   **ROME BEAUTY**
BALDWIN   **SPARTAN**

For lunchboxes and salads

RED DELICIOUS   **GOLDEN DELICIOUS**

3 MEDIUM APPLES = 1 POUND
3 MEDIUM APPLES
PEELED AND SLICED = 2¾ CUPS
1 AVERAGE APPLE = 80 CALORIES

Taste your apples and add a little less sugar to recipes for very sweet apples, and a little more for tart. You really can't go wrong with apples!

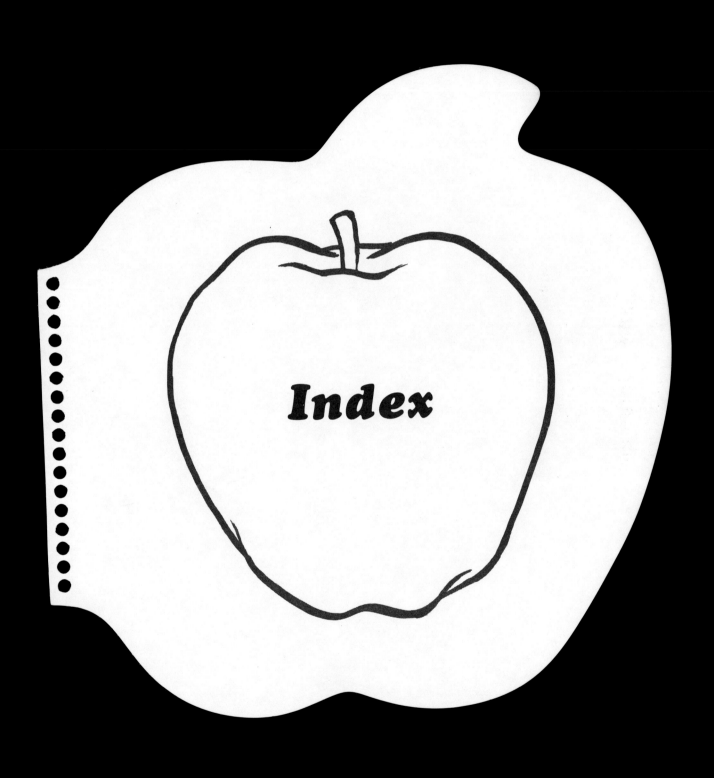

Index

Salads

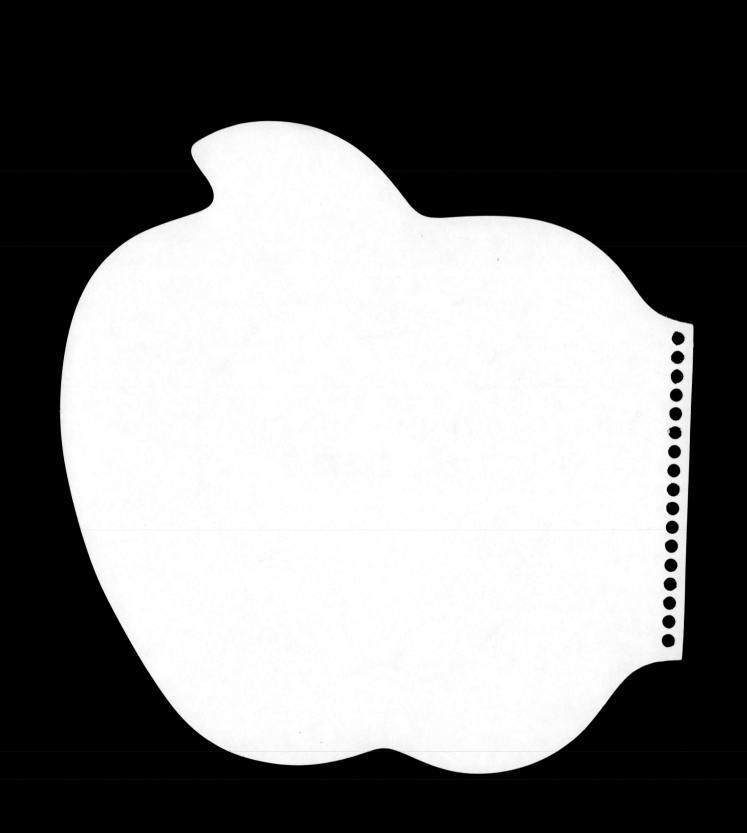

1 Cinnamon Applesauce Salad

Our all time family favorite, so pretty in a ring mold with a cottage cheese center. Great for the little ones.

1 pkg red gelatin
2 T red cinnamon candies
1 C boiling water
¼ C cold water
2 C applesauce

Dissolve candies in boiling water, add gelatin and stir to dissolve. Add cold water and applesauce. Chill in a ring mold. Unmold and fill center with cottage cheese.

2 Applesauce Pineapple Salad

Make it in a minute!

1 C applesauce
1 small pkg red gelatin
1 small can 7Up
1 6½ oz can drained
  crushed pineapple
Nuts, if desired

Dissolve gelatin in applesauce that has been heated to boiling. Add rest of ingredients and chill until set. Serves 6.

3 Apple-Cabbage Mold

Cool and crunchy

1 3oz pkg lemon gelatin
2 C hot water
½ C shredded cabbage
4 t vinegar
½ t salt
1 C diced unpeeled apple
¼ C chopped walnuts

Dissolve gelatin in water according to package directions. Chill until slightly thickened. Combine cabbage, vinegar and salt, and let stand 20 minutes. Fold cabbage, apples and nuts into gelatin and turn into oiled mold. Chill until set. Unmold on crisp lettuce.

4 Apple-Cranberry Relish

For Thanksgiving and Christmas

1 pkg fresh cranberries
2 unpeeled large, sweet apples
2 large peeled oranges
peel of ½ orange
1-1½ C sugar

Put all fruits and peel through a grinder or food processor. Add sugar to taste. Refrigerate for several hours. Serve as a sauce with ham, turkey, or as a salad.

5 Favorite Salad

Halved grapes, pineapple chunks and lettuce may be added to this classic mixture

2 C unpeeled sweet apples
1 C diced celery
½ C nutmeats
⅓ C mayonnaise
1 t sugar
1 T milk

Cut apples in bite-sized pieces. Add celery and nuts. Blend mayonnaise with sugar and milk, and stir gently into apple mixture. Serve on lettuce leaves. Serves 6.

6 Dessert Apple Salad

At our house this is "Grandma's Apple Salad"

4 C peeled diced apple (any variety)
1 C miniature marshmallows
sweetened whipped cream, or dessert topping
sugar to taste, depending on sweetness of apple

Mix together to desired consistency, and chill. Garnish with Maraschino Cherries. Serves 12.

7 Fresh Fruit Salad

A sprinkle of coconut on top is nice

2 unpeeled sweet apples
2 bananas
2 peeled oranges
½ C sugar (or less)
1 T cornstarch
1 C apple cider or may use orange juice

Cut fruits in bite-sized pieces. Combine sugar, cornstarch and juice in a sauce pan. Cook until thickened. Cool and mix with fruits. 8-12 servings.

8 Apple-Grape Salad

A delicious combination with cream cheese

1 3 oz pkg lime gelatin
1 3 oz pkg cream cheese
2 C boiling water
1 C diced apple, peeled otr unpeeled
1 C miniature marshmallows
½ C halved green grapes
nuts, if desired

Dissolved gelatin in 1 C boiling water. Pour remaining 1 cup boiling water over cheese cut into chunks. Combine and refrigerate until mixture is partially set. Add apple, marshmallows, grapes, and nuts. Chill until set. 8-10 servings.

9 Summer Salad

2 C diced unpeeled apples
2 C diced peeled cucumbers
½ t salt
3 T lemon juice
½ C mayonnaise
¼ C chopped dry-roasted nuts
lettuce leaves

Mix apple, cucumbers and nuts. Add salt and lemon juice to mayonnaise. Mix lightly into apple mixture. Serve chilled on lettuce.

10 Apple-Banana Salad

The peanuts add a nice crunch

4 sweet apples, 2 red, 2 yellow, unpeeled
2 bananas
½ C dry-roasted peanuts
½ C mayonnaise
2 T honey (or 2 T sugar)
2 T orange juice

Cut apples in bite-sized pieces and combine with sliced bananas and nuts. Mix mayonnaise, honey and juice. Combine lightly with fruit. Serve on lettuce leaves. Serves 4-5 as a main dish.

11 Layered Applesauce Salad

Pretty enough for a centerpiece

1 C boiling water
2 T red cinnamon candies
1 3 oz pkg red gelatin
1½ C applesauce
1 8 oz pkg cream cheese
½ C chopped nuts
½ C celery, sliced
½ C mayonnaise

Dissolve candies in hot water, add gelatin and stir until dissolved. Stir in applesauce. Pour ½ of mixture into oiled mold, and chill. Blend softened cream cheese, nuts, celery and mayonnaise. Spread cheese over firm gelatin in mold. Pour remaining apple mixture on top and chill until set. Unmold to serve. 8 servings.

12 Apples 'N Chicken Salad

A natural go-together

4 C diced, cooked chicken breast
1 C diced unpeeled red apple
1 C sliced celery
1 C pineapple tidbits
1 C halved green grapes
Mayonnaise
Lettuce leaves

Combine apple with drained pineapple. Add chicken, celery and grapes. Add just enough mayonnaise to hold ingredients together. Chill. Serve on lettuce leaves. Serves 10-12.

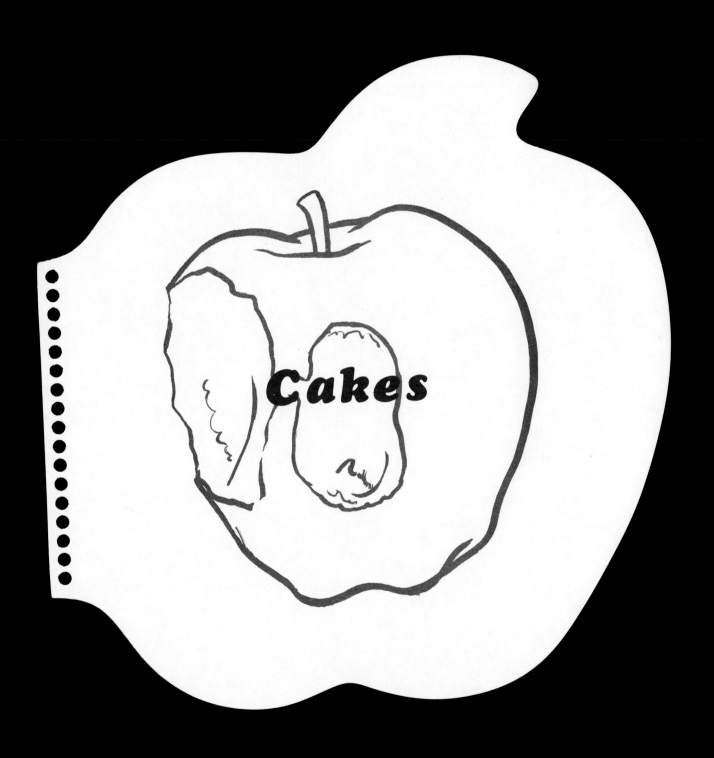

Cakes

13 Applesauce Picnic Cake

Makes any meal a picnic

1½ C sugar
½ C shortening
2 eggs
1½ C applesauce
2 C flour
3 T cocoa
1½ t soda
1½ t salt
1 t each cinnamon, cloves, nutmeg
½ C water
1 C chocolate bits

Cream sugar with shortening; add eggs, beating until light. Stir in applesauce. Mix cocoa with flour and spices; add alternately with water to creamed mixture. Spread batter in oiled 13x9 cake pan. Sprinkle raw batter with chocolate chips. Bake at 350 degrees, 35-40 minutes or until cake tests done. Cool and serve with whipped topping.

14 Apple Date Cake

Ever have a date with an apple?

½ C shortening
¾ C sugar
1 egg
1½ C flour
1 t soda
2 C apple, peeled and chopped
1 8 oz pkg dates, diced
¼ C brown sugar
1 t cinnamon
½ C nuts

Cream shortening and sugar, add egg. Mix flour, soda and salt, and add alternately with apple and dates. Pour batter into an oiled 9x9 pan. Mix brown sugar, cinnamon and nuts and spread over batter. Bake at 350 degrees, 35 minutes. Serve with whipped topping.

15 Apple Butter Bundt Cake

1 pkg yellow cake mix
½ C finely chopped nuts
1 C peeled diced apple
1 C dairy sour cream
⅓ C apple butter
4 eggs

Filling: 1 C chopped nuts
2 T brown sugar
2 t cinnamon

Glaze: 1 C powdered sugar
2-3 T apple butter

Blend all cake ingredients and beat for 2 minutes. Pour ⅓ of batter in prepared bundt pan; sprinkle with ½ the filling; and repeat these two layers. Cover with remaining batter. Bake at 325 degrees, 50-55minutes. Cool in pan and invert on serving plate. Spoon glaze over cake.

16 Cider Cake

After a trip to the cider mill

3 C sifted cake flour
1 T baking power
¾ t salt
1 t cinnamon
1 t nutmeg
¼ t cloves

¾ C shortening
1⅓ C brown sugar
3 eggs
1 T lemon juice
1 C cider

Cream shortening and sugar; add beaten eggs. Mix cider and lemon juice; add alternately with dry ingredients. Bake in three greased 8" layer cake pans at 350 degrees for 25-30 minutes. Cool. Fill and frost with cider filling and icing.

17 Cider Cake Filling

½ C sugar
¼ t salt
3 T cornstarch

1 C cider
2 T lemon juice
1 T butter

Mix sugar, salt and cornstarch. Heat cider and lemon juice; when hot, stir in sugar mixture and cook until thickened and clear. Add butter. Cool before spreading on cake.

18 Cider Icing

½ C melted butter
3½ T flour
¼ t salt

½ C cider
3 C powdered sugar
½ C chopped nuts

Blend flour and salt into melted butter in a sauce pan. Add cider, bring to a boil and cook for 1 minute. Add sugar and beat until smooth. Add nuts and spread on cake.

19 Apple Pecan Cake

Great picnic fare

6 T shortening
⅓ C brown sugar
⅔ C white sugar
2 eggs
2 C flour
1 t baking powder
1 t salt
½ t soda
1 C milk
1½ C finely chopped apple

Topping
⅓ C brown sugar
½ C broken pecans
2 T melted butter

Cream brown sugar, white sugar and shortening. Add eggs and beat until light. Add dry ingredients alternately with milk, and mix just until blended. Fold in apple. Spread batter in oiled 8x8 pan; sprinkle with brown sugar and nutmeats. Drizzle melted butter over all. Bake at 350 degrees, 25-30 minutes.

20 Apple Walnut Cake

With Lemon Butter Icing

1½ C sugar
4 C peeled, chopped apple
2 eggs
½ vegetable oil
2 t vanilla
2 C sifted flour
2 t baking powder
2 t cinnamon
1 t salt
1 C chopped walnuts

Combine apples and sugar and let stand. Beat eggs, oil and vanilla. Stir dry ingredients into egg mixture alternately with apple. Stir in walnuts. Bake at 350 degrees 1 hour or until cake tests done.

Lemon Butter Icing

3 C confectioners sugar
2 T lemon juice
¼ t salt

If icing is too thick to spread, add a few drops of water.

21 Apple Upside Down Cake I

4 T butter
½ C brown sugar
½ t cinnamon
3 large apples
1 t lemon juice
pecan halves

Melt butter in a 9x9 baking pan. Add brown sugar and cinnamon. Arrange peeled, sliced apples and pecans over sugar, and sprinkle with lemon juice.

Batter:

½ C sugar
1 egg
4 T shortening
1¼ C flour
1½ t baking powder
½ t salt
½ C milk

Cream sugar and shortening, and add egg. Stir in dry ingredients and milk at once, stirring only until blended. Do not overbeat. Pour over apples in pan. Bake at 350 degrees, 30 minutes or until cake tests done. Invert hot cake on cake plate. Serve warm with whipped topping.

22 Apple Upside Down Cake II

A larger cake, pretty and spicy

4 large apples, peeled and sliced
1 C cider or apple juice
⅓ C butter
1 C brown sugar
1 pkg spice cake mix
Maraschino cherries
½ C walnut meats (optional)

Cook apples in apple juice for 5 minutes or until tender. Drain and reserve juice. Melt butter in 13x9 cake pan. Add ¼ cup apple juice, brown sugar and apples. Decorate with cherries and nuts. Prepare cake according to package directions, using remaining apple juice for part of the liquid. Pour batter over apples. Bake at 350 degrees for 30-40 minutes or until cake tests done. Invert hot cake on platter.

23 German Applesauce Cake

1 C sugar
½ C shortening
2 eggs
1½ C applesauce
1 C raisins
½ C chopped nuts

2 C flour
½ t cloves
1 t cinnamon
2 t soda dissolved in 1 T water
Topping:
¼ c sugar
1 t cinnamon

Cream shortening and sugar; add eggs and beat until light. Add applesauce and soda alternately with dry ingredients. Stir in raisins and nuts. Pour batter into a prepared 9x13 pan. Mix sugar and cinnamon topping and sprinkle over batter. Bake at 350 degrees, 25 minutes or until done.

24 Cocoa Applesauce Cupcakes

A Halloween treat for little goblins.

1 C sugar
¼ C margarine
1 egg
1½ C applesauce

1½ C flour
½ C cocoa
2 t baking soda
1 t vanilla

Cream sugar and margarine; add egg and vanilla; beat until light. Add flour to creamed mixture alternately with applesauce. bake in muffin tins lined with cupcake papers 12-15 minutes at 375 degrees. Frost with white icing, and decorate with candy corn. 1½ dozen cupcakes.

25 Diabetic Apple Cake

2½ C flour
3 t soda
2 t cinnamon
½ t nutmeg
1 t salt
1 C butter

2 t vanilla
2 eggs
1 t liquid sugar substitute
4 C grated apple
1 C walnuts

Mix dry ingredients; add butter, vanilla, eggs, sugar substitute, and blend well. Stir in grated apples and nuts. bake in well-greased 9x13 pan at 375 degrees, 40-45 minutes. (1 serving equals ½ fat exchange, 1 bread, ½ fruit)

26 Applesauce Meringue Cake

A company treat.

1½ C sugar
½ C shortening
2 egg yolks
1½ c unsweetened
  applesauce
2 t soda

3 C flour
1 C chopped nuts
1 t lemon extract
2 egg whites
⅔ C brown sugar

Cream shortening and sugar; add egg yolks and lemon extract. Mix soda with flour and nuts; add to creamed mixture alternately with applesauce. Pour batter into a greased 9x13 pan. Beat egg whites until stiff; gradually beat in brown sugar. Spread meringue over raw cake batter. Bake at 350 degrees, 30-40 minutes or just until cake tests done. Do not overbake.

27 White Apple Brownies

That's right, there is no leavening

⅔ C butter or margarine
1 C brown sugar
1 C white sugar
2 eggs
1 t vanilla

2 C sifted flour
½ t salt
½ C chopped nuts
½ C chopped apple

Cream butter, sugar and eggs; add dry ingredients. Stir in apple and nuts. Bake in a greased 8x12 pan, 30-35 minutes. Do not over bake. Cut in bars. When cool, roll in powdered sugar.

28 Chocolate Apple Brownies

½ C butter or margarine
2 squares unsweetened
chocolate
2 eggs
1 C sugar
1 C flour

½ t baking powder
¼ t salt
1 C nutmeats
1 C chopped apple
1 t vanilla

Melt butter and chocolate over low heat. Beat eggs and add sugar. Stir in chocolate mixture and beat well. Stir in dry ingredients, then apples, nuts and vanilla. Bake in a greased 8 inch square pan at 350 degrees for 25-30 minutes. Cool. Dust with powdered sugar.

29 Apple Bars

Beware of theft with these

2¼ C flour, divided
1¼ C sugar, divided
½ t baking powder
½ t salt
1 C butter or margarine
2 egg yolks

4 C sliced apple
1 t cinnamon
1 C powdered sugar
1½ T milk

Combine 2 C of the flour, ½ C sugar, baking powder and salt. Cut in butter until crumbs are the size of peas. Stir in egg yolks. Press half of mixture into bottom of a 9x13 pan, and reserve the rest. Combine apples, remaining flour, sugar and cinnamon; place apple mixture over crust in pan. Sprinkle with remaining crumbs. Bake at 350 degrees 40-45 minutes. Cool and drizzle with thin icing of powdered sugar and milk. Three dozen three inch bars.

30 Applesauce Raisin Cookies

Naturally sweetened with raisins—no sugar

2 C raisins
2 C water
1 C unsweetened
applesauce
1 t vanilla
¾ C vegetable oil
2 t liquid sugar substitute
2 eggs

2 C flour
½ t salt
1 t baking soda
½ t nutmeg
½ t cinnamon
4 T carob powder or cocoa
½ C nuts

Simmer raisins in water until water is absorbed. Add applesauce, vanilla, oil, sweetener and eggs to cooled raisins. Stir in dry ingredients and nuts. Mix well. Drop by spoonfuls on greased baking sheets and bake at 350 degrees, 15-20 minutes, just until done. Do not overbake.

31 Spiced Apple Cookies

A surprising ingredient

3 C flour
2 t baking soda
1½ t cinnamon
1 t allspice
1 C chopped apples
1 C raisins

1½ C brown sugar
2 eggs
1 can tomato soup
½ t cloves
½ C butter or margarine

Stir together flour, baking soda,and spices. In large bowl of electric mixer, beat butter and sugar, add eggs and soup. Gradually blend in flour mixture. Stir in remaining ingredients. Drop by teaspoon on greased cookie sheet. Bake for 10 minutes in 350 degree oven. May frost if desired with cream cheese icing.

32 Applesauce Cookies

¾ C soft shortening
1 C brown sugar
1 egg
½ C applesauce
2¼ C flour
(nuts optional)

½ t soda
½ t salt
¾ t cinnamon
¼ t cloves
1 C raisins

Mix shortening, sugar and egg thoroughly. Stir in applesauce and dry ingredients. Add raisins and nuts. Drop on greased cookie sheet. Bake for 10-12 minutes in 375 degree oven.

33 Apple Oatmeal Cookies

½ C butter
1 C brown sugar
2 eggs
1¾ C flour
½ C rolled oats
½ t salt

2 t baking powder
½ t cinnamon
1 C raisins
1 C walnuts
1¾ C finely chopped apples

Cream butter with sugar; add eggs, beat until light. Combine all remaining ingredients and stir into the creamed mixture. Drop on oiled baking sheet and bake 12-15 minutes at 350 degrees.

34 Applesauce Oatmeal Cookies

Sweet and spicy with no sugar

1 C unsweetened
applesauce
¼ lb. margarine, melted
3 t liquid sweetener
1 egg
1 t vanilla
½ t cinnamon
½ t nutmeg

½ t cloves
1½ C flour
½ t baking soda
½ C oatmeal
½ C raisins
½ C chopped nuts

Pour boiling water over raisins to plump them, then drain off water and discard. Mix applesauce, margarine, sweetener, egg and vanilla with raisins. Mix in dry ingredients. Drop on greased cookie sheets. Bake at 350 degrees, 12-15 minutes.

35 Apple Nuggets

Super! Everything in 'em

1 C shortening
1½ C brown sugar
¼ C molasses
3 eggs
3½ C flour
½ t salt
1 t baking soda

3 t cinnamon
½ t cloves
½ t nutmeg
1 C chopped peanuts
1 C chopped apple
6 oz. pkg chocolate chips

Cream shortening and sugar; add eggs and molasses. Add dry ingredients. Stir in peanuts, apple and chocolate chips. Mix well. Drop on greased baking sheet. Bake at 350 degrees, 12-15 minutes. Make about 5 dozen.

36 Apple Butter Cookies

2 C brown sugar
½ C shortening
2 eggs
1 C oatmeal
1 C apple butter

1 C chopped nuts
3 C flour
6 T milk
2 t baking powder
2 t baking powder

Cream butter and sugar; add eggs, oatmeal and apple butter. Mix dry ingredients together and add alternately with milk. Fold in nuts. Drop on greased cookie sheets and bake at 400 degrees for 10-12 minutes.

37 Apple Pancakes

Dust with powdered sugar and add a dollop of apple jelly

1½ C flour
1¼ t baking powder
½ t salt
½ t nutmeg
⅓ C sugar

1 egg
1 C milk
¼ C melted butter
1 C apple, finely chopped

Combine egg, milk and apple; stir into dry ingredients. Stir in melted butter. Bake on a hot griddle. 12 pancakes.

38 Apple Corn Muffins

1 C yellow corn meal
1½ C flour
½ C brown sugar
½ t salt
3 t baking powder

2 apples, finely chopped
1 egg
1 C milk

Mix dry ingredients; combine milk and egg and stir into dry mixture. Fold in apple. Spoon into greased or sprayed muffins cups. Bake at 400 degrees, 20-25 minutes. Do not overbake. 12 muffins.

39 Applesauce Nut Bread

2 C flour	½ t cinnamon
¾ C sugar	1 egg
3 t baking powder	1 C applesauce
1 t salt	2 T oil
½ t soda	1 C chopped nuts

Beat egg, add applesauce and oil. Combine dry ingredients and nuts and add to applesauce mixture. Stir just until blended. Pour into greased loaf pan and bake at 350 degrees for one hour. Cool and sprinkle top with powdered sugar.

40 Quick Apple Honey Buns

2 loaves frozen bread dough
1 C brown sugar
½ C honey
3 T butter

Filling:
4 T melted butter
½ C applesauce
2 T brown sugar
¼ C raisins

Put both frozen loaves in a plastic bag. Let thaw and rise until double in size. Mix brown sugar, honey and 3 T butter. Spread in bottom of 13x9 pan. Roll dough in a rectangle. Combine filling ingredients and spread on dough. Roll up as for jelly roll and slice 1 inch thick. Place slices in pan. Let rise for 20 minutes. Bake at 350 degrees, 20 minutes. Cool and frost with powdered sugar icing. 1 dozen rolls.

41 Apple Oatmeal Loaf

½ C milk or buttermilk
¼ C water
2 T butter
1 pkg hot roll mix
½ t salt

¼ C sugar
¾ C diced unpeeled apple
½ C oatmeal
1 egg

Glaze: 1 C powdered sugar, 1-2 T milk

Heat milk, water and butter until very warm. Dissolve yeast from roll mix in milk mixture. Stir in all ingredients except flour and mix well. Stir in flour and blend. Cover and let rise until doubled. Stir down dough and spoon into a greased loaf pan. Cover and let rise again. Bake at 350 degrees, 30-35 minutes. Remove from pan and glaze if desired.

42 German Fresh Apple Bread

Dark and tender

1 C flour
1 t baking soda
½ t salt
½ t cinnamon
½ C shortening
1 C sugar
2 eggs

1 C dark and tender apple, finely chopped
1½ T evaporated milk
½ t vanilla
1 C chopped nuts
Topping:
1 T sugar
1¼ t cinnamon

Cream shortening and sugar; add eggs and mix well. Stir in apples, milk and vanilla. Mix dry ingredients together then stir into batter. Do not overbeat. Fold in nuts. Pour mixture into a greased bread loaf pan. Sprinkle topping over raw batter. Bake at 350 degrees, 50-60 minutes.

43 Spiced Apple Muffins

2 C flour
3 t baking powder
1 t salt
5 T sugar
1 t nutmeg

1 egg
1 C milk
3 T oil
1 C finely chopped apple

Combine dry ingredients; add oil, egg and milk and stir just until blended. Fold in apple. Fill greased muffin cups ⅔ full. Bake at 400 degrees, 20-25 minutes.

44 Spicy Apple Coffee Cake

Cinnamon topping:

1¼ C flour
½ t salt
1 T brown sugar
1 t baking powder
½ C butter or margarine
1 egg yolk
2 T milk
2 apples, peeled
¼ C golden raisins

½ C sugar
2 T flour
½ t cinnamon
¼ t ginger
¼ t cloves
¼ t nutmeg
2 T butter

Combine flour, salt, brown sugar and baking powder; cut in butter with a pastry blender. Combine egg yolk and milk; stir into flour mixture until blended. Press mixture into the bottom and one inch up sides of a nine inch round cake pan. Cut apples in large slices and arrange on dough in pan. Sprinkle with raisins, then with cinnamon topping. Bake at 350 degrees, 45 minutes.

Main Dishes

45 Chicken-Apple Pot Pie

Also good with turkey

2 C cubed peeled apple
¼ C chopped onion
2 T butter
2 cans chicken soup
2 C cubed cold chicken
⅓ C raisins (optional)
¼ t nutmeg
Pastry for a one crust pie

Saute onion in butter until golden. Mix with remaining ingredients and put in an oiled casserole or loaf dish. Top with crust. Cut vent holes in crust. Bake at 425 degrees, 30 minutes.

46 Pork Loin with Apples

Elegant!

2 lb. boned rolled loin of pork
salt
freshly ground black pepper
2 T water
4-5 tart cooking apples
¼ C hard cider or wine

2 T cream

Place pork in oiled roasting pan, sprinkle with salt and pepper. Add water. Roast at 375 degrees 1¾ hrs, basting often. Peel, core and quarter apples. Remove meat from pan and drain off cooking juices. Pour cider into pan, add pork, surround with apples, dot with butter. Roast 20 minutes more, or until pork is tender. Transfer pork and apples to platter. Stir cream into pan juices and cook on top of stove for two minutes, stirring constantly. Pour sauce over apples. Serves 6-8.

47 Apple-Stuffed Acorn Squash

A good combination

3 medium acorn squash
½ C butter or margarine, melted and divided
salt
ground cinnamon
3 apples, peeled, cored, and chopped
1 T grated lemon rind
1 T lemon juice
½ C honey

Wash squash, cut in half lengthwise and remove seeds. Place squash, cut side down, in a 13x9 baking dish. Add ½ inch water and bake at 375 degrees for 35 minutes. Turn cut side up and brush cut surfaces and cavities with 2 T butter. Sprinkle lightly with salt and cinnamon. Combine apples, lemon rind, lemon juice, remaining 2 T butter, and honey. Mix well and spoon into squash cavities. Bake at 350 degrees, 30 minutes.

48 Apple-Sauerkraut Casserole

An unbeatable combination

2 lb. sauerkraut, rinsed and drained
3 peeled, sliced apples
¼ C raisins (optional)
1 lb. sweet sausage, cooked and drained
¼ C water
2 T honey

Alternate layers of kraut, apple, sausage and raisins in an oiled casserole dish. Add water and drizzle with honey. Bake at 350 degrees, 1 hour.

49 Hot Applesauce and Sausage

Brown link sausages in electric fry pan. Pour off fat. Cover with applesauce and simmer 30 minutes. Serve with pancakes or waffles.

50 Applesauce Meat Loaf

1 lb. ground beef
1 egg, beaten
2 T chopped onion
1 t salt

½ C bread or cracker crumbs
½ C applesauce
2 T catsup

Combine ingredients and mix well with hands. Put in a greased loaf pan. Spread catsup on top of loaf. Bake at 400 degrees, 45 minutes. Serve with additional applesauce.

51 Spicy Apples and Rice

Serve with pork chops or pork steak

1 large tart apple, unpeeled, chopped
½ C chopped onion
½ C chopped celery
1 T butter
3 C cooked rice
1 T brown sugar
¼ t allspice
½ C raisins
½ C sliced almonds

Pour boiling water over raisins and let stand to plump them, then drain. Cook celery and onion in butter until tender crisp. Stir in spices, rice and raisins. Heat thoroughly. Add apple, cover and let stand 5 minutes. Sprinkle with almonds. Serves 6.

52 Skillet Dinner

1 large apple, diced
½ lb. sweet sausage

1 –2 can sauerkraut
3-4 T sour cream

Cook sausage in skillet, remove from pan and drain on paper towels. Remove all but one tablespoon of grease from pan. Add apple and sauerkraut which has been rinsed and drained. Fry on low until mixture is lightly browned and apple is cooked. Lightly combine sausage and sour cream with mixture and serve. Serves 4.

53 Fried Apples and Carrots

To surround a platter of roast pork

6 tart apples
2 T margarine
1 t salt

6 medium carrots
1 T sugar

Scrape carrots and cut in lenghtwise slices. Slice unpeeled, cored apples in crosswise slices. Melt margarine in a large fry pan. Place carrots and apples in a pan in a single layer. Cover and cook until browned. Turn and brown other side. Just before they are done, sprinkle with sugar and salt.

54 Fried Apples

Serve for breakfast with an omelet

4 green apples   2 T butter or bacon fat

Core the unpeeled apples and cut crosswise into ½ inch slices.
Cook in butter or bacon fat (adds flavor) until soft. Serve.

If you prefer a sweeter fruit, sprinkle apples in skillet with ¼ C
brown sugar, and 2 T water. Continue cooking until apples are
coated with syrup.

55 Glazed Apples and Sweet Potatoes

2 large apples   3 T butter
4 medium sweet potatoes   ⅓ C molasses
½ t salt   ¼ C brown sugar
2 t lemon juice   ¼ C chopped nuts

Boil sweet potatoes until tender, but still firm, and allow to cool.
Then peel, slice, and place potatoes in a shallow casserole dish.
Peel and slice apples; sprinkle with salt and lemon juice. Fry
apples in hot butter until slightly soft; arrange apple slices in dish
with potatoes. Add molasses to butter in pan and bring to a boil.
Pour over casserole; sprinkle with brown sugar and nuts. Bake at
325 degrees, 30 minutes. Serves 4-6.

56 Apple Casserole

2 unpeeled red apples, sliced
3 C shredded cabbage
1 lb. ham, cut in chunks
½ C cracker crumbs
sweet and sour sauce

Cook cabbage until almost tender; place in 1 qt. casserole with apples. Add meat and cover with sweet and sour sauce. Dot with butter. Bake covered at 350 degrees, 30 minutes. Uncover and bake 15 minutes more.

Sweet and Sour sauce

2 T butter
¼ C brown sugar
½ C water

¼ C vinegar
¾ t salt
2 T cornstarch

Mix sugar and cornstarch, blend into melted butter. Add rest of ingredients and cook until thick and clear.

57 Cider Stew

Cider adds the zip

1 lb. stewing beef
3 t flour
3 T oil
1 t salt
½ t pepper
1 t allspice

1-2 C cider
2 T catsup
2 large onions
3 large potatoes
2 large carrots
2 stalks celery

Place flour, salt, pepper and allspice in a plastic bag. Shake beef a few pieces at a time in a bag to coat. Brown meat in oil; add cider and catsup. Cover and cook slowly 1-1½ hours or until meat is tender. Cut onions, potatoes, carrots and celery into bite-sized chunks; add to meat and simmer 30 minutes more. Thicken stew if desired. Serve with hot biscuits. Serves 6.

58 Old Fashioned Apple Pie

Like Grandma made it

5-6 large cooking apples
¾ C sugar ' 1 T
2 T flour
1 t cinnamon
1 T butter
pastry for 2 crusts

Slice apples to fill pie pan. Transfer to bowl and mix with sugar and cinnamon. Line pie pan with pastry. Sprinkle 1 T sugar and 1 T flour in bottom of pan and stir with fingers. Mix apples with ¾ C sugar and remaining flour. Pile in pie pan, and dot with butter. Wet edges of bottom crust with water, (makes crusts seal). Put on top crust and crimp. Sprinkle with sugar. Bake at 400 degrees, 40 minutes.

59 New Fashioned Apple Pie

1 9 inch unbaked pie shell	1 t cinnamon
6 tart apples	¼ C butter or oleo
¾ C sugar	½ C sour cream
⅓ C flour	

Slice apples into pie shell. Combine sugar, flour, and cinnamon; cut in butter, as for pie crust. Sprinkle this mixture over apples. Spoon sour cream on top and bake at 400 degrees, 15 minutes. Lower heat to 300 degrees for about 20 minutes or until apples are done.

60 Dutch Apple Pie

Irresistible with a slice of cheese!

1 unbaked pie shell	1 C flour
6 C sliced apples	½ C brown sugar
¾ C sugar	½ C butter or margarine
1 t cinnamon	

Mix apples with sugar and cinnamon and pile in pie shell. Mix flour, brown sugar and butter; press this topping on top of apples. Bake at 375 degrees, 35-40 minutes.

61 No Sugar Apple Pie

But sweet as pie!

6 large Red or Golden Delicious apples
½ t cinnamon
¼ t nutmeg
1 T flour
1 6 oz can frozen apple juice
1 T butter
Pastry for one or two crust pie

Peel and slice apples, sprinkle with flour and spices. Blend in thawed, undiluted juice. Put into bottom crust and dot with butter; or for a deep dish pie, put apple mixture in a loaf pan, dot with butter. Put on top crust, and cut air vents. Bake at 400 degrees, 40 minutes.

62 Cottage Apple Pie

2 eggs
¼ t salt
¾ C sugar, divided
½ C light cream
¾ C milk
1 t vanilla

1 C cottage cheese
1½ C sliced apples
¼ t cinnamon
¼ t nutmeg
1-10 inch unbaked pie shell

Combine eggs, ½ C sugar, salt, cream, milk, vanilla, and cottage cheese. Set aside. Combine apples, ¼ C sugar and spices in pie shell. Bake at 425 degrees, 15 minutes. Reduce heat to 325 and add custard mixture. Bake 40 minutes longer.

63 Apfelkuchen

Crust:
4 T butter
1 T sugar
1 T vinegar
1 C flour

Filling:
5-6 tart cooking apples
¾ C sugar
1 T butter
¼ t cinnamon

Mix crust ingredients, cutting butter and vinegar into flour and sugar with a pastry blender. Press mixture into a pie pan as for pie crust. Mix filling ingredient, put in crust and dot with butter. Bake 15 minutes at 400 degrees, 35 minutes at 350 degrees.

64 Sour Cream Apple Pie

1 unbaked pieshell

Filling:
2 T flour
¾ C sugar
1 egg, unbeaten
1 C sour cream
1 t vanilla
¼ t nutmeg
3 C finely chopped apple

Topping:
⅓ C brown sugar
⅓ C flour
1 t cinnamon
¼ C butter

Mix egg, sour cream, vanilla and nutmeg; add flour and sugar that has been mixed. Stir in apple. Pour mixture into pie shell and bake at 400 degrees for 30 minutes. Blend topping ingredients. Remove pie from oven and sprinkle topping over pie. Return to oven and bake 10 minutes more.

65 Hoosier Apple Pie

6 apples, sliced
⅔ C sugar
½ t cinnamon

1 T tapioca
1 C light cream
½ t salt

Fill unbaked 9 inch pie shell with mixture of apples, sugar, cinnamon, salt and tapioca. Pour cream over apples. Bake at 425 degrees, 40-50 minutes.

66 Deep-Dish Apple Pie

Serving a crowd? Make it in a cake pan and cut in squares

2 C flour
¾ C brown sugar
¾ C quick oatmeal
1 t salt
½ C shortening
¾ C sugar

1 T cornstarch
1 t cinnamon
1 C boiling water
1 T butter
6 large cooking apples
peeled and sliced

Combine flour, brown sugar, oatmeal, and salt in a bowl. Cut in shortening with a pastry blender. Reserving one cup, press remaining mixture into a 10 inch deep-dish pie plate. Combine sugar, cornstarch and cinnamon in a heavy saucepan. Stir in water and butter. Cook, stirring constantly for 3 minutes. Stir apples into hot mixture and pour into prepared pie plate. Top with reserved crumbs. Bake at 350 degrees, 50 minutes.

67 Apple-Molasses Pie

From the 1800's

4 c sliced apples
½ C molasses
¼ t nutmeg

½ C sugar
2 T butter
½ t cinnamon

Line a pie plate with pastry and fill with apples. Cover with sugar, pour on molasses, and dot with butter. Sprinkle on spices and cover with top crust. Bake at 375 degrees, 35-40 minutes.

68 Apple Scotch Pie

6-8 sliced apples
1 C water
4 T flour
2 T butter
Pastry for a 2 crust pie

1½ C brown sugar
2 t vinegar
¼ t salt
1 t vanilla

Mix one-half of the sugar with water and vinegar and bring to a boil. Add apples and simmer until nearly tender. Remove apples. Mix remaining sugar with flour and salt; add slowly to syrup and cook until thickened. Remove from heat, add butter and vanilla and cool. Fill pastry lined pan with apples. Pour in syrup. Put a lattice top crust on pie. Bake at 400 degrees, 20-25 minutes.

69 Western Apple Pie

Don't like cinnamon? This is for you.

6 Delicious apples
½ C sugar
1½ T flour
¾ t lemon extract
2 T butter
Pastry for a two crust pie

Mix apple slices with sugar and flour. Sprinkle lemon extract over fruit and mix lightly with a fork to distribute it evenly. Put apples in pie shell, dot with butter, and put on top crust. Sprinkle crust with white sugar. Bake at 400 degrees, 10 minutes, reduce heat and bake at 350 degrees until apples are done.

70 Favorite Baked Apples

A holiday "must" at our house

6 firm cooking apples	3 T butter
½-¾ C brown sugar	3 T syrup
1 T red cinnamon candies	

Wash and cut apples in half. Remove cores, but do not peel. Arrange apple halves cut side up in a flat baking dish, sprinkle with sugar, and candies, dot with butter and drizzle syrup over all. (May use maple syrup, pancake syrup or any flavored syrup for variety.) Bake uncovered at 350 degrees, 30-40 minutes.

71 Red Pop Apples

On a diet?

4 cooking apples peeled and quartered
1 T minute tapioca
2 C diet red pop

Simmer apples in pop until almost tender. Stir in tapioca and cook one minute. Cool and serve with low calorie whipped topping.

72 Apple Pizza

Try this for a brunch for a bunch

Crust:
2¾-3 C flour
1 pkg dry yeast
3 T sugar
½ t salt
½ C water
¼ C milk
¼ C butter or margarine
1 egg

Apple Topping:
2 T butter
2 large cooking apples
½ C sugar
2 T flour
1 t cinnamon

Peel and slice apples. Melt butter in skillet, add apples, sugar, flour, and cinnamon. Simmer 15 minutes, then cool. Continued next page.

Cheese topping:
4 oz cream cheese
2 T sugar
1 T lemon juice
¼ t nutmeg
Mix and set aside

Streusel topping:
⅓ C flour
⅓ C sugar
¼ C soft butter
Mix and set aside

Blend 1½ C flour, yeast, sugar and salt in a large mixer bowl. Heat water, milk and butter until very warm; add to flour mixture and beat three minutes. By hand, stir in enough flour to make a soft dough. Cover and let rise 15 minutes. Pat dough onto a large oiled pizza pan, forming a rim around the edge. Spread on cheese topping, then apple topping over cheese; sprinkle with streusel topping. Cover and let rise for 15 minutes. Bake at 375 degrees, 25-30 minutes. Serve warm or cold. Serves 16.

73 Red Cinnamon Crisp

Beautiful and Delicious!

4 C sliced apples
½ C hot water
2 T red cinnamon candies
¾ C sugar
½ C flour
4 T butter

Put apple in 8x8 baking pan, sprinkle with candies and pour on hot water. Mix sugar and flour; cut in butter and pat mixture on apples. Bake at 375 degrees, 30 minutes. Double recipe for 9x13 pan.

74 Apple-Cheese Torte

A simply delicious dessert for your gourmet dinner

1 stick butter or margarine
¾ C sugar, divided
1 t vanilla, divided
1 C flour
1 8 oz pkg cream cheese
1 egg

4 C thinly sliced apples
½ t cinnamon
½ C powdered sugar
2 T milk
2 T toasted, slivered almonds

Cream together: butter, ¼ C sugar and ½ t vanilla. Add flour, and when well blended, press mixture into bottom and 1½ inches up side of a 9" spring form pan. Beat cream cheese, ¼ C sugar, egg, ½ t vanilla until mixture is smooth. Pour into prepared crust. Toss apple slices lightly with ¼ C sugar and cinnamon. Layer evenly over cream cheese. Bake at 450 degrees, 10 minutes, then reduce oven to 400 and continue baking 30-45 minutes or until apples test done. Cool in pan, then remove sides of pan and place on serving plate. Combine powdered sugar and milk, and drizzle over torte. Garnish with almonds. Serves 10-12.

75 Apple Cream Squares

2 C flour
2 C brown sugar
½ C margarine
1 C chopped nuts
2 t cinnamon
1 t soda
½ t salt
1 C dairy sour cream
1 t vanilla
1 egg
3 C chopped apple

Blend flour, sugar and margarine until crumbly. Stir in nuts. Press 2¾ cups of mixture into bottom of a 13x9 baking pan. To rest of crumb mixture, add all other ingredients except apple and blend well. Stir in chopped apple, and spoon mixture evenly over crumb crust. Bake at 350 degrees, 25-35 minutes.

76 Apple Yum

All healthy stuff

4 C sliced apples	½ stick butter
2 t cinnamon	½ C whole wheat flour
1 T lemon juice	¼ C sesame seeds
¼ C honey	¼ C oatmeal
¼ C butter	¼ C cider

Place apples in a greased 9x9 baking pan. Sprinkle with cinnamon and lemon juice. Blend butter and honey; mix in rest of ingredients to make a crumbly topping. Put topping on apples and pour cider over all. Bake at 350 degrees, 35 minutes.

77 Apple Crisp I

8 C sliced tart apples
1 t cinnamon
1½ C sugar
1 C flour

1 t baking powder
1 egg
⅓ C melted butter

Place apples in oiled 3x9 pan. Sprinkle with ½ t cinnamon. Mix sugar, flour and baking powder. Stir egg into dry mixture with a fork. Spread the crumb mixture over apples. Pour melted butter over all and sprinkle with remaining cinnamon. Bake at 375 degrees, 40-45 minutes, or until apples are done.

78 Apple Crisp II

4 C tart cooking apples
¼ C white sugar
1 t cinnamon

¾ C brown sugar
½ C flour
½ stick melted butter

Slice apples into an oiled 9x9 pan, sprinkle with sugar and cinnamon. Mix brown sugar, flour and butter. Spread this crumbled mixture over apples. Bake at 375 degrees, 30-35 minutes.

79 Crock Pot Apple Pudding

The easiest steamed pudding ever!

2 C sugar
1 C oil
2 eggs
2 t vanilla
2 C flour

1 t soda
1 t nutmeg
2 C unpeeled apple, finely chopped
1 C chopped nuts

Beat sugar, oil, eggs, and vanilla. Add apple with dry ingredients and mix well. Spray a two pound coffee can with cooking spray or grease and flour it well. Pour batter into can, filling no more than ⅔ full. Place can in crock pot. Do not add water. Cover, but leave cover ajar so steam can escape. Cook on high 3½-4 hours. Don't peek before last hour of baking. Cake is done when top is set. Let stand in can a few minutes before tipping pudding out on a plate. Serve half-rounds plain, with whipped topping, or a pudding sauce.

80 Apple Dumplings I

Made the easy way

4 C sliced apples
⅔ C brown sugar
½ C honey

½ C water
1 t cinnamon
Dumplings from biscuit mix

Combine apples, sugar, honey, and water in an electric frying pan. Cook 10 minutes. Follow recipe for dumplings on a package of biscuit mix. Drop from spoon on apples in pan, and sprinkle with cinnamon; cover and cook for 12 minutes on medium, or until dumplings are done. Put warm dumplings in dessert dishes and spoon apples and syrup over them.

81 Apple Dumplings II

Made the hard way, but worth it for "your" dumplings

Pastry for a two crust pie
4 medium sized appples
⅓ C sugar
1 t cinnamon
4 t butter

Syrup:
⅔ C brown sugar (may use white)
1½ C water
2 T butter
¼ t cinnamon

Roll out pastry as for pie and cut in 7 inch squares. Peel and core apples, but leave whole. Place an apple on each square of dough and fill cavity with sugar, cinnamon and 1 t butter. Bring opposite points of dough up to overlap apple. Moisten to seal. Place dumplings in a baking dish. Heat syrup to boiling. Pour hot syrup around dumplings and bake at 400 degrees, 40-45 minutes or until apples are done.

82 Apple Graham Cracker Pudding

Have a child who helps you cook? Try this.

12 single graham crackers
8 medium apples
⅓ C sugar
1 t cinnamon
2 C milk

Crumble six graham crackers in the bottom of a greased 1½ qt. casserole dish. Cover with half of the apples; sprinkle with cinnamon and sugar. Repeat this layer and pour milk over all. Bake at 350 degrees, 30-40 minutes or until apples are tender. Serve warm with milk or whipped topping.

83 Apple Rice Pudding

A very old, delicious concoction

1 C cooked rice
1 C unsweetened
applesauce
1 C brown sugar
¾ t vanilla

⅓ C water
1 T flour
2 T melted butter

Mix all ingredients and bake in a 1 qt casserole 350 degrees, 25 minutes.

84 Apple Pinwheels

2 C flour
1 T sugar
2 t baking powder
½ t salt
3 T shortening
4 cooking apples
½ C brown sugar

1 t cinnamon
2 T butter
Syrup:
1 C sugar
1 C cider or apple juice
1 T flour
¼ t salt

Combine flour, 1 T sugar, baking powder and salt; cut in shortening. Stir in milk to make a soft dough. Roll out dough on a floured board to a 16X10 rectangle. Top with apples, brown sugar and cinnamon. Dot with butter. Roll up jelly roll fashion, and cut in two inch slices. Place slices in a greased 13X9 baking pan. Syrup: Combine sugar, flour and salt. Heat cider or juice and stir in sugar mixture. Cook until slightly thickened and pour carefully over pinwheels. Bake at 350 degrees, 40 minutes. Serves 8.

85 Birds Nest Pudding

Don't ask me why it's called that. I don't know. But it's good.

1 egg
2 T sugar
½ t salt
½ C cream
½ C milk
2 C flour
4 t baking powder

5-6 medium apples
1 t cinnamon

Topping: (after baking)
1 T butter
½ C sugar

Put thinly sliced apples in a buttered deep pie dish; sprinkle with cinnamon. Blend the egg, sugar, salt, cream, milk, flour and baking powder just until mixed. Shape dough with hands to cover apple dish. Bake at 400 degrees, 25 minutes. When done, invert pudding on a plate; spread butter over hot apples, and sprinkle with sugar. Cut in wedges and serve warm with cream.

86 Apple Brown Betty

A big hit

4 C fresh whole-wheat
bread crumbs
½ C melted butter
1 C sugar
2 t cinnamon

10-12 apples
1 lemon
1 C orange juice
light cream, or whipped topping

Toss bread crumbs with melted butter. Grate lemon rind, and squeeze juice from lemon; combine lemon juice and rind, sugar and cinnamon. Peel and slice apples. In a 13X9 cake pan, layer: crumbs, apples and sugar and repeat, ending with crumbs. Pour orange juice evenly over top. Bake covered at 350 degrees, 30 minutes, Uncover and bake 15 minutes more. Serve hot or cold with cream or whipped topping.

87 Apple Shortcake

Make the shortcake while the apples stew

5 medium apples
⅓ C raisins
⅔ C sugar
1 t cinnamon
½ C water

2 C flour
3 t baking powder
1 t salt
2 T sugar
⅔ C milk
⅓ C oil

Combine peeled, sliced apples with raisins, sugar, cinnamon and water; cook just until apples are tender. Remove from heat. Mix milk with oil; stir into dry shortcake ingredients just until flour is dampened. Pat dough ¾ inch thick and cut biscuits with a floured glass. Bake shortcakes at 450 degrees, 10-12 minutes or until golden. Spoon warm apples over buttered hot shortcakes. Serves 6.

88 Rice-Raisin-Apple Pudding

Thanks to Bernadette...

6 C sliced apples
½ C raw rice
¼-⅓ C dark raisins
2 T butter

⅔ c sugar
1 t cinnamon
3 C milk (approximately)

In a greased 2 quart casserole, layer: rice, raisins, apples, sugar and cinnamon. Repeat layer. Pour on milk almost to the top of apples. Dot with butter. Cover and bake at 325 degrees, 1 hour. This may also be cooked in a heavy sauce pan on top of stove, by using low heat, and a trivet to prevent burning.

89 Butterscotch Apples

6 baking apples
⅓ C light cream
⅓ C dark corn syrup
⅓ C chopped pecans

Sauce:
1 C light cream
⅓ C dark corn syrup
 2 T butter
1 t vanilla

Wash and core apples, but do not peel; place in a buttered shallow baking dish. Combine cream, syrup and pecans and fill center of apples. Bake at 350 degrees until tender. Combine sauce ingredients and simmer 20-30 minutes until thickened. Arrange warm apples on a plate with dessert dish of warm sauce in center. Serves 6.

90 Candied Apple Rings

The perfect garnish for holiday meat platters

2 C sugar
1 C water
⅓ C red cinnamon candies
whole cloves

firm apples, peeled and cored
and sliced crosswise in ½ in rings

Make syrup in a fry pan. Cook the apple slices in syrup turning often until tender and transparent. (Watch carefully). Remove to a deep platter with slotted spoon. Pour remaining syrup over apples. Chill.

91 Apple Fritters

1 C flour
1½ t baking powder
¼ C sugar
1¼ t salt
1 T oil

1 egg beaten
⅓ C milk
2 large apples peeled, sliced in eighths
powdered sugar

Combine dry ingredients, add egg, milk and oil. Beat batter until smooth. Dip apples in batter and fry in deep fat, 4 minutes or until brown. Dust with powdered sugar.

92 Applesauce

8 apples
½ C water
½ C sugar

¼ t salt
¼ t nutmeg

Quarter apples, remove cores and cook in skins in water. Put
through a food mill to remove skins; OR, peel and core apples, and
simmer in the water until tender. Stir in sugar, salt and nutmeg
and simmer one minute longer. Adjust sugar for sweetness of
apple.

93 Baked Applesauce with Cider

8-10 apples
1 C brown sugar
½ t nutmeg

1 C cider
2 T lemon juice

Peel and quarter apples and place in a casserole dish. Heat
sugar, cider, lemon juice and nutmeg until sugar is dissolved. Pour
cider over apples. Cover and bake at 350 degrees, 30-35 minutes
until apples are soft. Stir with a fork before serving. Serve warm
or cold.

94 Cider Fruit Soup

½ C dried apples
½ C dried apricots
¼ C dark raisins
¼ C golden raisins
1 cinnamon stick

4 C apple cider
2 C water
2 C mixed fresh fruit
in season; strawberries, grapes
plums, blueberries, etc.

Put apples, apricots and raisins and cinnamon stick in a saucepan with water and cook slowly ½ hour, or until soft. Place half of mixture in a blender and puree. Return to saucepan, add cider and reheat. When hot, add fresh fruits and cook for 5-8 minutes. Remove from heat. This nectar can be served hot as a sauce, or chilled as an appetizer.

95 Freezing Cider

You can enjoy fresh apple cider from your freezer all winter long if you follow simples rules.

Pour about 1 C of cider from each gallon jug to allow for expansion in freezing. It is better to freeze cider in plastic jugs. To thaw, leave at room temperature or in refrigerator until completely thawed. Do not pour out liquid while there is still unmelted ice. Shake well. (May also thaw in microwave oven.)

96 Perked Cider

Enough for a crowd!

2 gallons cider (more or less)
3 sticks cinnamon, broken
1 t whole cloves
½ t whole allspice

Pour cider in a 30 cup electric coffee maker. Put spices in basket. Perk through the cycle as for coffee. Keep hot and serve from the spigot. (Spices can be saved, added to and reused once.)

97 Cider Punch

2 quarts lemon sherbet
1 gallon cider
1 large bottle gingerale
lemon slices

Pour cider over sherbet in punch bowl. Add gingerale. Float lemon slices on top.

98 Apple Warm-Up

1 qt. cider
¼ C instant tea powder
½ C lemon juice
¼ C sugar
1¼ C red fruit punch
2 C water

Combine ingredients and heat through. Serve in mugs with an apple slice.

99   Easy Hot Cider

Buy the oils at the drug store and make it in a minute!

Pour the desired amount of cider in crock pot and turn on low. Add:

4 drops oil of cinnamon
4 drops oil of cloves

Use these amounts for full crock pot and decrease acccordingly. Float thin slices of lemon and/or orange on top and cover. Heat for one hour after cider is hot before serving. May be kept on low for many hours.

100   Hot Cider and Spice

Fill crock pot with cider. Sprinkle in ½ t pumpkin pie spice. Decrease spice accordingly for a lesser quantity. Heat for one hour after cider is hot. May be kept hot on low setting for several hours.

101 Wassail

2 qts. cider
2 C cranberry juice
¾ C sugar
2 pieces stick cinnamon

1½ t whole allspice
1 orange studded with whole cloves
1 C rum (optional)

Combine all ingredients in a slow cooker and brew for 4-5 hours before serving.

102 Mulled Cider

2 qts. cider
½ C brown sugar
1 t whole allspice

1½ t whole cloves
2 pieces stick cinnamon
orange slices

Mix cider and sugar in a crock pot or slow cooker. Put spices in a tea ball or tie in cheese cloth, add to cider. Heat on high for 1 hour, and brew on low for 2-3 hours before serving. May keep at serving temperature for many hours. Serve with a ladle.

Miscellaneous

103 Grandma's Mincemeat

Homemade mincemeat need not be a treat from the past. Don't let the amounts or ingredients scare you off. Have a party and have each guest bring an ingredient. Grind and mix it together and let everyone take a panful home to bake and freeze. It is guaranteed to become a yearly event.

7 lbs. meat, ½ beef, ½ pork, may also use venison. Any quality or cut of meat can be used, even ground meat.
½ bushel apples
1 box seedless raisins
1 box seeded raisins
2 boxes currants
5 lbs. sugar
2 qts. canned or frozen sour cherries (add sugar for frozen)
1½ qt. cider
½ C vinegar
1½ T black pepper (yes, that's right)
1½ T salt
1½ T cinnamon
1½ t ground cloves
May add some tart jelly if desired

Cook meat until tender, cool, remove fat and bones and grind. Grind cored, unpeeled apples. Mix everything together well. Simmer until everything is thoroughly cooked. Baking in a moderate oven works well. May be canned or frozen. Use in pies, cookies, or any recipe calling for mincemeat.

104 Apple Peanut Butter Fudge

1 6 oz pkg chocolate chips 1 t vanilla
½ jar marshmallow creme 2 C sugar
½ C peanut butter ⅔ C cider

Combine first four ingredients in a bowl. Cook sugar and cider over moderate heat to soft ball stage (240 degrees). Remove from heat and quickly add chocolate mixture. Stir until blended. Pour into a 9 inch buttered pan. Cool and cut in squares.

105 Grilled Caramel Apples

Spear apple through stem end on a long fork or skewer. Lay apple on grill or hold over coals. Roast, turning now and then until skin breaks and may easily be pulled off. Peel, dip in bowl of melted butter and twirl immediately in brown sugar. Hold apple over grill until it is covered with a rich caramel coating. Don't burn it or YOU! May also dip caramel apple in chopped nuts.

106 Cinnamon Apple Jelly

A perfect Christmas gift!

1 qt cider
1 pkg pectin
4½ C sugar
⅓ C red cinnamon candies

Combine cider, pectin and candies in large saucepan. Bring to a full boil. Add sugar, bring to a full boil and boil two minutes. Remove from heat and skim off foam. Pour into jelly glasses and seal with paraffin.

107 Caramel Apples

12 medium red apples
12 wooden skewers
1 lb. light colored caramels
¼ C evaporated milk or cream

Wash, dry and skewer apples on sticks. Melt caramels and cream together in microwave oven or over hot water. Plunge apples in syrup and twist to coat evenly. Place on wax paper covered cookie sheet in refrigerator for 2 hours.

108 Fried Apple Sandwiches

Spread one side of bread with apple butter. Spread second slice with pimento cheese and sprinkle with nuts. Put slices together and butter outside. Toast in skillet as for toasted cheese sandwiches.

109 Apple Pickles

2 C peeled apples, quartered
1 C vinegar
¼ t cloves
1 stick cinnamon
2 C sugar

Boil all ingredients together except apples for 5 minutes. Add apples and cook until tender. Refrigerate. Excellent served with pork.

110 Apple Butter

5 lbs. tart apples (about 10 large apples)
2 C cider
sugar
¾ t cloves
½ t allspice
3 t cinnamon
½ t nutmeg

Wash, quarter and remove stems from apples. No need to peel or core. Cook apples slowly in cider until tender and put through a food mill. Add ½-⅔ C sugar for each cup of apple pulp. Add spices. Cook in the oven or in a slow cooker for several hours, stirring often. Test for desired thickness by spooning some of mixture on a cold plate. When no liquid oozes around edges, it is thick enough. May be canned while hot, or frozen.

111 Canned Apple Pie Filling

Do all the peeling at once! A quart makes a pie.

1 grocery sackful of apples (Ida Red is my
preference), peeled, cored and sliced for pie

10 C water
5 C white sugar
1 C cornstarch
5 t cinnamon
2 T lemon juice

Wash and scald quart jars (or let your dishwasher do it for you).
Fill jars full of apples. Combine syrup ingredients and bring to a
boil. Pour syrup to tops of jars. Seal and process for 20 minutes in
a hot water bath.

112 Apple Snack

For holiday snacking

2½ C dried apples
10 C popped popcorn
2 C pecan halves
4 T butter

1 t cinnamon
¼ t nutmeg
2 T brown sugar
¼ t vanilla

Preheat oven to 250 degrees. Place apples in a single layer in a large, flat baking pan. Bake for 20 minutes. Remove from oven and stir in popcorn and pecans. Mix remaining ingredients in a cup and drizzle over apples, popcorn and nuts. Return to oven and bake for 30 minutes, stirring every 10 minutes.

THE BIG FAT RED JUICY APPLE COOK BOOK makes a nice hostess, birthday, or shower gift for an apple lover. Order extra copies now to have on hand, or let us send your gift for you! (We will enclose a gift card)

L.E.B. Inc.
27599 Schoolcraft
Livonia, Michigan 48150

YES! Please send _____ Apple cook book(s) @ $6.95 + $1.00 postage and handling to:

_____

NAME _____
                          Please Print

ADDRESS _____

CITY _____ STATE _____ ZIP _____

Enclose a gift card from: _____ *your name*

....

YES! Please send _____ Apple cook book(s) @ $6.95 + $1.00 postage and handling per book to:

_____

NAME _____
                          Please Print

ADDRESS _____

CITY _____ STATE _____ ZIP _____

Enclose a gift card from: _____ *your name*